twenty 20

January
S	M	T	W	T	F	S
			1	2	3	4
5	6	7	8	9	10	11
12	13	14	15	16	17	18
19	20	21	22	23	24	25
26	27	28	29	30	31	

February
S	M	T	W	T	F	S
						1
2	3	4	5	6	7	8
9	10	11	12	13	14	15
16	17	18	19	20	21	22
23	24	25	26	27	28	29

March
S	M	T	W	T	F	S
1	2	3	4	5	6	7
8	9	10	11	12	13	14
15	16	17	18	19	20	21
22	23	24	25	26	27	28
29	30	31				

April
S	M	T	W	T	F	S
			1	2	3	4
5	6	7	8	9	10	11
12	13	14	15	16	17	18
19	20	21	22	23	24	25
26	27	28	29	30		

May
S	M	T	W	T	F	S
					1	2
3	4	5	6	7	8	9
10	11	12	13	14	15	16
17	18	19	20	21	22	23
24	25	26	27	28	29	30
31						

June
S	M	T	W	T	F	S
	1	2	3	4	5	6
7	8	9	10	11	12	13
14	15	16	17	18	19	20
21	22	23	24	25	26	27
28	29	30				

July
S	M	T	W	T	F	S
			1	2	3	4
5	6	7	8	9	10	11
12	13	14	15	16	17	18
19	20	21	22	23	24	25
26	27	28	29	30	31	

August
S	M	T	W	T	F	S
						1
2	3	4	5	6	7	8
9	10	11	12	13	14	15
16	17	18	19	20	21	22
23	24	25	26	27	28	29
30	31					

September
S	M	T	W	T	F	S
		1	2	3	4	5
6	7	8	9	10	11	12
13	14	15	16	17	18	19
20	21	22	23	24	25	26
27	28	29	30			

October
S	M	T	W	T	F	S
				1	2	3
4	5	6	7	8	9	10
11	12	13	14	15	16	17
18	19	20	21	22	23	24
25	26	27	28	29	30	31

November
S	M	T	W	T	F	S
1	2	3	4	5	6	7
8	9	10	11	12	13	14
15	16	17	18	19	20	21
22	23	24	25	26	27	28
29	30					

December
S	M	T	W	T	F	S
		1	2	3	4	5
6	7	8	9	10	11	12
13	14	15	16	17	18	19
20	21	22	23	24	25	26
27	28	29	30	31		

January

January
2020

Monthly Goals

Monthly Snapshot

Top Priorities

TASKS & NOTES

January 2020

SUNDAY	MONDAY	TUESDAY	WEDNESDAY
			1
5	6	7	8
12	13	14	15
19	20	21	22
26	27	28	29

Fresh OUT OF Fucks

January 2020

THURSDAY	FRIDAY	SATURDAY	Shit-To-Do List
2	3	4	○
			○
			○
			○
			○
9	10	11	○
			○
			○
			○
16	17	18	○
			○
			○
			○
			○
23	24	25	○
			○
			○
			○
			○
30	31		NOTES

January
2020

01 WEDNESDAY
-
-
-
-
-
-
-
-

02 THURSDAY
-
-
-
-
-
-
-
-
-
-

03 FRIDAY
-
-
-
-
-
-
-
-

04 SATURDAY
-
-
-
-
-

January 2020

05 SUNDAY
-
-
-
-
-
-
-
-

06 MONDAY
-
-
-
-
-
-
-
-

07 TUESDAY
-
-
-
-
-
-
-
-

08 WEDNESDAY
-
-
-
-
-

January 2020

09 THURSDAY

10 FRIDAY

11 SATURDAY

12 SUNDAY

13 MONDAY

14 TUESDAY

15 WEDNESDAY

16 THURSDAY

17 FRIDAY

18 SATURDAY

19 SUNDAY

20 MONDAY

January 2020

21 TUESDAY

22 WEDNESDAY

23 THURSDAY

24 FRIDAY

January 2020

25 SATURDAY

26 SUNDAY

27 MONDAY

28 TUESDAY

January 2020

29 WEDNESDAY

30 THURSDAY

31 FRIDAY

NOTES

February

February

2020

Monthly Goals

Monthly Snapshot

Top Priorities

TASKS & NOTES

February 2020

SUNDAY	MONDAY	TUESDAY	WEDNESDAY
2	3	4	5
9	10	11	12
16	17	18	19
23	24	25	26

I have 3 moods: **WHAT THE FUCK?** | **ARE YOU FUCKING KIDDING ME.** | **FUCK THIS SHIT!**

February 2020

THURSDAY	FRIDAY	SATURDAY	Shit-To-Do List
		1	○
			○
			○
			○
			○
6	7	8	○
			○
			○
			○
13	14	15	○
			○
			○
			○
			○
20	21	22	○
			○
			○
			○
			○
27	28	29	NOTES

February
2020

01 SATURDAY

02 SUNDAY

03 MONDAY

04 TUESDAY

February 2020

05 WEDNESDAY

06 THURSDAY

07 FRIDAY

08 SATURDAY

February 2020

09 SUNDAY

10 MONDAY

11 TUESDAY

12 WEDNESDAY

February 2020

13 THURSDAY

14 FRIDAY

15 SATURDAY

16 SUNDAY

February 2020

17 MONDAY

18 TUESDAY

19 WEDNESDAY

20 THURSDAY

21 FRIDAY

22 SATURDAY

23 SUNDAY

24 MONDAY

February 2020

25 TUESDAY

26 WEDNESDAY

27 THURSDAY

28 FRIDAY

29 SATURDAY

NOTES

March

2020

Monthly Goals

Monthly Snapshot

Top Priorities

TASKS & NOTES

March 2020

SUNDAY	MONDAY	TUESDAY	WEDNESDAY
1	2	3	4
8	9	10	11
15	16	17	18
22	23	24	25
29	30	31	

I'm sorry. It's just that I literally **DON'T GIVE A FUCK**

March 2020

THURSDAY	FRIDAY	SATURDAY	Shit-To-Do List
5	6	7	○ ○ ○ ○ ○
12	13	14	○ ○ ○ ○
19	20	21	○ ○ ○ ○ ○
26	27	28	○ ○ ○ ○ ○
			NOTES

March
2020

01 SUNDAY

02 MONDAY

03 TUESDAY

04 WEDNESDAY

March 2020

05 THURSDAY
-
-
-
-
-
-
-
-

06 FRIDAY
-
-
-
-
-
-
-
-

07 SATURDAY
-
-
-
-
-
-
-
-

08 SUNDAY
-
-
-
-
-

09 MONDAY

10 TUESDAY

11 WEDNESDAY

12 THURSDAY

March 2020

13 FRIDAY

14 SATURDAY

15 SUNDAY

16 MONDAY

March 2020

17 TUESDAY

18 WEDNESDAY

19 THURSDAY

20 FRIDAY

March 2020

21 SATURDAY

22 SUNDAY

23 MONDAY

24 TUESDAY

March 2020

25 WEDNESDAY

26 THURSDAY

27 FRIDAY

28 SATURDAY

March
2020

29 SUNDAY

30 MONDAY

31 TUESDAY

NOTES

April

2020

Monthly Goals

Monthly Snapshot

Top Priorities

TASKS & NOTES

April 2020

SUNDAY	MONDAY	TUESDAY	WEDNESDAY
			1
5	6	7	8
12	13	14	15
19	20	21	22
26	27	28	29

 Four drinks in and I'm using **FUCK** like a comma

April 2020

THURSDAY	FRIDAY	SATURDAY	Shit-To-Do List
2	3	4	○
			○
			○
			○
			○
9	10	11	○
			○
			○
			○
16	17	18	○
			○
			○
			○
			○
23	24	25	○
			○
			○
			○
			○
30			NOTES

More Shit To Do

April 2020

01 WEDNESDAY

02 THURSDAY

03 FRIDAY

04 SATURDAY

05 SUNDAY

06 MONDAY

07 TUESDAY

08 WEDNESDAY

09 THURSDAY

10 FRIDAY

11 SATURDAY

12 SUNDAY

13 MONDAY

14 TUESDAY

15 WEDNESDAY

16 THURSDAY

April 2020

17 FRIDAY

18 SATURDAY

19 SUNDAY

20 MONDAY

April 2020

21 TUESDAY

22 WEDNESDAY

23 THURSDAY

24 FRIDAY

April 2020

25 SATURDAY

26 SUNDAY

27 MONDAY

28 TUESDAY

29 WEDNESDAY

-
-
-
-
-
-
-
-

30 THURSDAY

-
-
-
-
-
-
-
-

NOTES

May

2020

Monthly Goals

Monthly Snapshot

Top Priorities

TASKS & NOTES

May 2020

SUNDAY	MONDAY	TUESDAY	WEDNESDAY
3	4	5	6
10	11	12	13
17	18	19	20
24	25	26	27

Inhale the GOOD SHIT   Exhale the BULL SHIT

May 2020

THURSDAY	FRIDAY	SATURDAY	Shit-To-Do List
	1	2	○
			○
			○
			○
			○
7	8	9	○
			○
			○
			○
14	15	16	○
			○
			○
			○
			○
21	22	23	○
			○
			○
			○
			○
28	29	30 / SUNDAY 31	NOTES

More Shit To Do

May
2020

01 FRIDAY
-
-
-
-
-
-
-
-

02 SATURDAY
-
-
-
-
-
-
-
-
-

03 SUNDAY
-
-
-
-
-
-
-
-
-

04 MONDAY
-
-
-
-
-

May 2020

05 TUESDAY

06 WEDNESDAY

07 THURSDAY

08 FRIDAY

May 2020

09 SATURDAY

10 SUNDAY

11 MONDAY

12 TUESDAY

May 2020

13 WEDNESDAY

14 THURSDAY

15 FRIDAY

16 SATURDAY

17 SUNDAY

18 MONDAY

19 TUESDAY

20 WEDNESDAY

May
2020

21 THURSDAY

22 FRIDAY

23 SATURDAY

24 SUNDAY

May 2020

25 MONDAY

26 TUESDAY

27 WEDNESDAY

28 THURSDAY

May 2020

29 FRIDAY

30 SATURDAY

31 SUNDAY

NOTES

June

2020

Monthly Goals

Monthly Snapshot

Top Priorities

TASKS & NOTES

june 2020

SUNDAY	MONDAY	TUESDAY	WEDNESDAY
	1	2	3
7	8	9	10
14	15	16	17
21	22	23	24
28	29	30	

I'm not always a BITCH. Just kidding, go FUCK YOURSELF.

June 2020

THURSDAY	FRIDAY	SATURDAY	Shit-To-Do List
4	5	6	○
			○
			○
			○
			○
11	12	13	○
			○
			○
			○
18	19	20	○
			○
			○
			○
			○
25	26	27	○
			○
			○
			○
			○
			NOTES

More Shit To Do

June 2020

01 MONDAY

02 TUESDAY

03 WEDNESDAY

04 THURSDAY

June 2020

05 FRIDAY

06 SATURDAY

07 SUNDAY

08 MONDAY

June 2020

09 TUESDAY

10 WEDNESDAY

11 THURSDAY

12 FRIDAY

June 2020

13 SATURDAY

14 SUNDAY

15 MONDAY

16 TUESDAY

June 2020

17 WEDNESDAY

18 THURSDAY

19 FRIDAY

20 SATURDAY

21 SUNDAY

22 MONDAY

23 TUESDAY

24 WEDNESDAY

June 2020

25 THURSDAY

26 FRIDAY

27 SATURDAY

28 SUNDAY

June 2020

29 MONDAY

30 TUESDAY

NOTES

July

2020

Monthly Goals

Monthly Snapshot

Top Priorities

TASKS & NOTES

July 2020

SUNDAY	MONDAY	TUESDAY	WEDNESDAY
			1
5	6	7	8
12	13	14	15
19	20	21	22
26	27	28	29

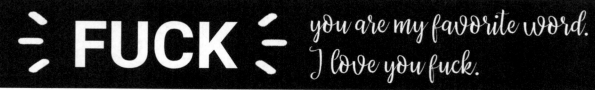

FUCK you are my favorite word. I love you fuck.

July 2020

THURSDAY	FRIDAY	SATURDAY	Shit-To-Do List
2	3	4	○
			○
			○
			○
			○
9	10	11	○
			○
			○
			○
16	17	18	○
			○
			○
			○
			○
23	24	25	○
			○
			○
			○
			○
30	31		NOTES

July
2020

01 WEDNESDAY

02 THURSDAY

03 FRIDAY

04 SATURDAY

July
2020

05 SUNDAY

06 MONDAY

07 TUESDAY

08 WEDNESDAY

July 2020

09 THURSDAY

10 FRIDAY

11 SATURDAY

12 SUNDAY

July 2020

13 MONDAY

14 TUESDAY

15 WEDNESDAY

16 THURSDAY

July 2020

17 FRIDAY

18 SATURDAY

19 SUNDAY

20 MONDAY

July 2020

21 TUESDAY

22 WEDNESDAY

23 THURSDAY

24 FRIDAY

July 2020

25 SATURDAY

26 SUNDAY

27 MONDAY

28 TUESDAY

July 2020

29 WEDNESDAY

30 THURSDAY

31 FRIDAY

NOTES

August

2020

Monthly Goals

Monthly Snapshot

Top Priorities

TASKS & NOTES

August 2020

SUNDAY	MONDAY	TUESDAY	WEDNESDAY
2	3	4	5
9	10	11	12
16	17	18	19
23 / 30	24 / 31	25	26

I don't have a short temper. I just have a quick reaction to **BULLSHIT.**

August  2020

THURSDAY	FRIDAY	SATURDAY	Shit-To-Do List
		1	○
			○
			○
			○
			○
6	7	8	○
			○
			○
			○
13	14	15	○
			○
			○
			○
			○
20	21	22	NOTES
27	28	29	

August
2020

01 SATURDAY

02 SUNDAY

03 MONDAY

04 TUESDAY

August
2020

05 WEDNESDAY

06 THURSDAY

07 FRIDAY

08 SATURDAY

August 2020

09 SUNDAY

10 MONDAY

11 TUESDAY

12 WEDNESDAY

August 2020

13 THURSDAY

14 FRIDAY

15 SATURDAY

16 SUNDAY

August 2020

17 MONDAY

18 TUESDAY

19 WEDNESDAY

20 THURSDAY

August 2020

21 FRIDAY

22 SATURDAY

23 SUNDAY

24 MONDAY

August 2020

25 TUESDAY

26 WEDNESDAY

27 THURSDAY

28 FRIDAY

August 2020

29 SATURDAY

30 SUNDAY

31 MONDAY

NOTES

September

September

2020

Monthly Goals

Monthly Snapshot

Top Priorities

TASKS & NOTES

September 2020

SUNDAY	MONDAY	TUESDAY	WEDNESDAY
		1	2
6	7	8	9
13	14	15	16
20	21	22	23
27	28	29	30

 It's not my job to blow sunshine up your **ASS.**

September 2020

THURSDAY	FRIDAY	SATURDAY	Shit-To-Do List
3	4	5	○ ○ ○ ○ ○
10	11	12	○ ○ ○ ○
17	18	19	○ ○ ○ ○ ○
24	25	26	○ ○ ○ ○ ○
			NOTES

September
2020

01 TUESDAY

02 WEDNESDAY

03 THURSDAY

04 FRIDAY

September
2020

05 SATURDAY

06 SUNDAY

07 MONDAY

08 TUESDAY

September
2020

09 WEDNESDAY

10 THURSDAY

11 FRIDAY

12 SATURDAY

September 2020

13 SUNDAY

14 MONDAY

15 TUESDAY

16 WEDNESDAY

September 2020

17 THURSDAY

18 FRIDAY

19 SATURDAY

20 SUNDAY

September
2020

21 MONDAY

22 TUESDAY

23 WEDNESDAY

24 THURSDAY

September 2020

25 FRIDAY

26 SATURDAY

27 SUNDAY

28 MONDAY

September 2020

29 TUESDAY

30 WEDNESDAY

NOTES

October

2020

Monthly Goals

Monthly Snapshot

Top Priorities

TASKS & NOTES

October 2020

SUNDAY	MONDAY	TUESDAY	WEDNESDAY
4	5	6	7
11	12	13	14
18	19	20	21
25	26	27	28

YOU CAN JUST *supercalifuckilistickissmyassadocious*

October 2020

THURSDAY	FRIDAY	SATURDAY	Shit-To-Do List
1	2	3	○
			○
			○
			○
			○
8	9	10	○
			○
			○
			○
15	16	17	○
			○
			○
			○
			○
22	23	24	○
			○
			○
			○
			○
29	30	31	NOTES

More Shit To Do

October
2020

01 THURSDAY

02 FRIDAY

03 SATURDAY

04 SUNDAY

October
2020

05 MONDAY

06 TUESDAY

07 WEDNESDAY

08 THURSDAY

October
2020

09 FRIDAY

10 SATURDAY

11 SUNDAY

12 MONDAY

October
2020

13 TUESDAY

14 WEDNESDAY

15 THURSDAY

16 FRIDAY

October
2020

17 SATURDAY

18 SUNDAY

19 MONDAY

20 TUESDAY

October
2020

21 WEDNESDAY

22 THURSDAY

23 FRIDAY

24 SATURDAY

October
2020

25 SUNDAY

26 MONDAY

27 TUESDAY

28 WEDNESDAY

October
2020

29 THURSDAY
-
-
-
-
-
-
-
-

30 FRIDAY
-
-
-
-
-
-
-
-

31 SATURDAY
-
-
-
-
-
-
-
-

NOTES

November
2020

Monthly Goals

Monthly Snapshot

Top Priorities

TASKS & NOTES

november 2020

SUNDAY	MONDAY	TUESDAY	WEDNESDAY
1	2	3	4
8	9	10	11
15	16	17	18
22	23	24	25
29	30		

Just chuck it in the **FUCK IT BUCKET** and move on.

November 2020

THURSDAY	FRIDAY	SATURDAY	Shit-To-Do List
5	6	7	○
			○
			○
			○
			○
12	13	14	○
			○
			○
			○
19	20	21	○
			○
			○
			○
			○
26	27	28	○
			○
			○
			○
			○
			NOTES

… More Shit To Do

November
2020

01 SUNDAY

02 MONDAY

03 TUESDAY

04 WEDNESDAY

November 2020

05 THURSDAY

06 FRIDAY

07 SATURDAY

08 SUNDAY

November
2020

09 MONDAY

10 TUESDAY

11 WEDNESDAY

12 THURSDAY

November 2020

13 FRIDAY

14 SATURDAY

15 SUNDAY

16 MONDAY

November
2020

17 TUESDAY

18 WEDNESDAY

19 THURSDAY

20 FRIDAY

November 2020

21 SATURDAY

22 SUNDAY

23 MONDAY

24 TUESDAY

November 2020

25 WEDNESDAY

26 THURSDAY

27 FRIDAY

28 SATURDAY

November
2020

29 SUNDAY
-
-
-
-
-
-
-
-

30 MONDAY
-
-
-
-
-
-
-
-

NOTES

December

2020

Monthly Goals

Monthly Snapshot

Top Priorities

TASKS & NOTES

December 2020

SUNDAY	MONDAY	TUESDAY	WEDNESDAY
		1	2
6	7	8	9
13	14	15	16
20	21	22	23
27	28	29	30

I will not slap that bitch. I will not slap that bitch. I will not slap that bitch. I will not slap that bitch. I will not slap that bitch.

December 2020

THURSDAY	FRIDAY	SATURDAY	Shit-To-Do List
3	4	5	○
			○
			○
			○
			○
10	11	12	○
			○
			○
			○
17	18	19	○
			○
			○
			○
			○
24	25	26	○
			○
			○
			○
			○
31			NOTES

More Shit To Do

December
2020

01 TUESDAY

02 WEDNESDAY

03 THURSDAY

04 FRIDAY

December
2020

05 SATURDAY

06 SUNDAY

07 MONDAY

08 TUESDAY

December
2020

09 WEDNESDAY

10 THURSDAY

11 FRIDAY

12 SATURDAY

December
2020

13 SUNDAY

14 MONDAY

15 TUESDAY

16 WEDNESDAY

December
2020

17 THURSDAY

18 FRIDAY

19 SATURDAY

20 SUNDAY

December 2020

21 MONDAY

22 TUESDAY

23 WEDNESDAY

24 THURSDAY

December
2020

25 FRIDAY

26 SATURDAY

27 SUNDAY

28 MONDAY

December
2020

29 TUESDAY
-
-
-
-
-
-
-
-

30 WEDNESDAY
-
-
-
-
-
-
-
-

31 THURSDAY
-
-
-
-
-
-
-
-

NOTES

CPSIA information can be obtained
at www.ICGtesting.com
Printed in the USA
LVHW100820241119
638068LV00033B/3481/P